DK

Eye Wonder

Reptiles

A PENGUIN COMPANY
LONDON, NEW YORK, MUNICH, PARIS,
MELBOURNE, DELHI

Contents

Written and edited by Simon Holland
Designed by Tory Gordon-Harris

Managing editor Sue Leonard
Managing art editor Rachael Foster
Jacket design Chris Drew
Picture researcher Jo Haddon
Production Kate Oliver
DTP designer Almudena Díaz
Consultant Barbara Taylor

First published in Great Britain in 2002 by
Dorling Kindersley Limited
80 Strand, London WC2R 0RL

2 4 6 8 10 9 7 5 3

Copyright © 2002 Dorling Kindersley Limited, London

ISBN 0-7513-2877-4

Colour reproduction by Colourscan, Singapore
Printed and bound in Italy by L.E.G.O.

see our complete
catalogue at
www.dk.com

The reptile house

Reptiles are scaly-skinned, "cold-blooded" creatures with a bony skeleton and a backbone. They live on land, in fresh water, and in the sea. There are four main groups of reptiles alive today.

Desert tortoises

Tortoises live on land. Turtles and terrapins live in the sea (salt water) or in rivers and ponds (fresh water).

The *Chelonia* group

Tortoises, turtles, and terrapins are known as *Chelonians*. All members of this group, or "order", have a body that is protected by a shell.

Squamata everywhere!

The *Squamata* order contains every single species of lizard and snake. It is by far the largest group of living reptiles. Amazingly, nearly all reptiles are lizards and snakes.

Snakes may have had legs for digging down, but now

All Crocodilian reptiles, like these crocodiles, have tough, armour-like skin covering their entire bodies.

The *Crocodilians*

Crocodiles, alligators, caimans, and gharials all belong to the *Crocodilia* group. Most make their homes in warm freshwater rivers, lakes, and swamps.

The world is home to about 6,500 different reptile species.

A rare breed

Today, there is only one species of reptile remaining in the *Rhynchocephalia* group – the tuatara. Tuataras are only found in one area of the world – a set of small islands off the coast of New Zealand.

they wriggle around.

COLD BLOOD?

Reptiles are known as cold-blooded creatures, but they do not always have chilly blood. An animal is "cold-blooded" if its body temperature changes depending on how hot or cold the surroundings are. Reptiles bask in sunlight to heat up. This keeps the body working well. If a reptile's body is not warm enough, its stomach cannot properly deal with (digest) its food.

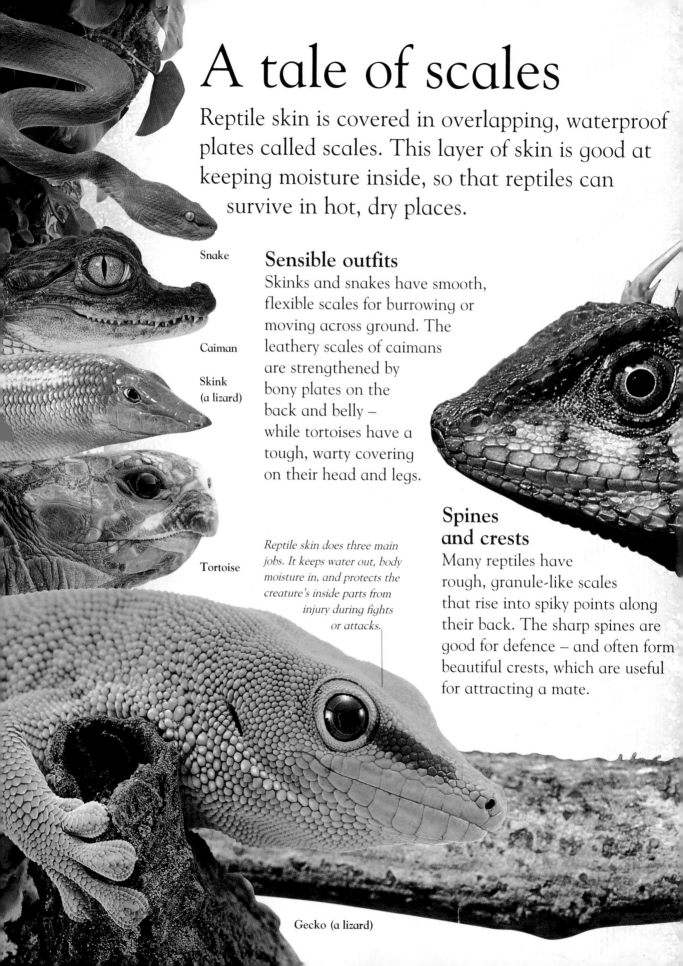

A tale of scales

Reptile skin is covered in overlapping, waterproof plates called scales. This layer of skin is good at keeping moisture inside, so that reptiles can survive in hot, dry places.

Snake

Sensible outfits

Skinks and snakes have smooth, flexible scales for burrowing or moving across ground. The leathery scales of caimans are strengthened by bony plates on the back and belly – while tortoises have a tough, warty covering on their head and legs.

Caiman

Skink
(a lizard)

Tortoise

Reptile skin does three main jobs. It keeps water out, body moisture in, and protects the creature's inside parts from injury during fights or attacks.

Spines and crests

Many reptiles have rough, granule-like scales that rise into spiky points along their back. The sharp spines are good for defence – and often form beautiful crests, which are useful for attracting a mate.

Gecko (a lizard)

Old skin, new skin

To get rid of older, worn-out scales, all reptiles shed their outer layer of skin from time to time. This is called moulting or sloughing. Snakes shed their whole skin in one piece, starting at the head end.

The snake's skin comes off inside out – like a sock being peeled off a human's foot.

This armoured spiny lizard has cone-like, spiky scales along the full length of its backbone (spine).

The skin of a reptile is not very good at holding on to body heat.

Reptile file

● A reptile's outer scales are mostly made up of something called keratin, which also goes into making human hair and fingernails.

● Lizards lose their skin bit by bit as it falls off in large flakes. Some peel it off with their mouth and eat it as food.

Scales are extra-thick pieces of skin.

Feeling the heat

Some snakes have special gaps around their lips that are sensitive to heat. These are called heat pits. They are used to detect warm-blooded animal prey.

This emerald tree boa has lots of heat pits along its lips.

Double vision

A chameleon can move one eye, on its own, without moving the other. This means that it can look in two different directions at the same time. It can use one eye to hunt insects, and the other to look out for attackers.

Reptile file

● Snakes do not have ears on the outside. They "hear" vibrations as they travel through their jaw bones and into their inner ears.

● The organ in snakes and lizards that "tastes" their environment is called the Jacobson's organ.

Sssenses

Most reptiles can see, hear, and smell, but they also have other ways of detecting things. Some reptiles rely on one sense that is very well-developed, while others use a mixture of sense skills to get by.

The taste test

A snake's tongue flicks in and out to collect up chemicals in the air. A sense organ inside the mouth "smells" and "tastes" these chemicals, helping the snake to sample food, find a mate, and to detect prey or enemies.

Snakes use their senses of smell, taste, and touch more than their eyesight and hearing.

Fully aware

Iguanas have very clear sight and full-colour vision. Like most lizards, they detect sounds in the air using an eardrum in the skin behind the eye.

The eardrum is very thin and flexible.

The body heat of this rat can be sensed by a snake's heat pits.

Slither slither

Along with lizards, snakes are members of the *Squamata* group. Snakes do not have hands and feet. Instead, they have a bendy body, which they use to wriggle and crawl over land – as well as for swimming through water. Their scales help them to grip surfaces.

Stretch marks
A snake's skeleton is simply a skull and a long, flexible backbone with ribs attached. Muscles joined to the ribs allow the snake to twist and coil its long, stretchy body.

Worried rattlesnakes raise their tails...

"Buzz" off
This western diamondback rattlesnake has a poisonous bite, but it does not like to waste its venom (poison). It always uses its rattle first, hoping that this will be enough to scare off its enemy.

The vines are alive!

Green tree snakes have light, skinny bodies for creeping and climbing. Their skin colour helps them to hide among green vines and foliage as they hunt for birds or tree-dwelling frogs and lizards.

The great pretender

The milksnake (right) is harmless, but has the same set of colours as the venomous coral snake (above). Predators get confused and so prefer not to attack.

Without venom, the milksnake has to strangle (constrict) its prey.

and twitch the tip to rattle out a warning "buzz".

Rubber-necks

Many snakes eat hard-shelled birds' eggs or soft-shelled reptile eggs. The African egg-eating snake only eats birds' eggs. It can unhook its jaws to swallow eggs that are at least twice the size of its head.

The stranglers

Some snakes – such as boas, pythons, and anacondas – capture and kill their prey by wrapping themselves around the animal until it can no longer breathe. These snakes are known as constrictors.

Friend or foe?

Some Burmese pythons live quite close to humans. Often, they attack farm animals – but their feeding habits can also help to control the number of rats, and other vermin, in villages and cities.

Burmese pythons can grow up to 6 m (20 ft) long.

Tropical living

Most species of boa live in the warm areas of Central and South America. This Cook's tree boa is a large, tree-dwelling snake found only in the Caribbean islands.

After a good feed, some constrictors can go for weeks without eating.

Killer coils

Constrictors catch and grip tightly on to their prey using sharp, curved teeth. They then coil themselves around the animal, and tighten their grip each time the victim breathes out.

Victims of constrictors die from either lack of air (suffocation) or shock.

The jaws stretch open and "walk" over the prey to force it, whole, down the boa's throat.

Anacondas are a type of boa. They live in South America, in rivers such as the Amazon.

A watery grave

Anacondas lurk in swamps and slow-moving rivers, waiting to catch birds – like this unlucky ibis – turtles, caimans, and mammals such as capybaras. Green anacondas can occasionally overpower and eat people.

Reptile file

- It often takes several days for a constrictor to digest its meal.

- The green anaconda is probably the largest snake in the world. Its body is so heavy that it finds it hard to move around on land.

Keen on greens

A cactus may not seem like the tastiest of snacks, but the Galápagos land iguana is very fond of the fleshy stems and fruits it finds on this kind of plant. The plant's prickly spines pass through the iguana's insides without harming the animal.

The tip of the tongue is covered in a sticky mucus that traps the insect.

Let's do lunch

Most lizards are swift, agile predators that feed on small animals, such as insects, mammals, birds, and other reptiles. Only a very small number of lizards, including large iguanas and skinks, snack on plants and fruits.

A chameleon's tongue is as long as the rest of its body.

A sticky end

Chameleons are mainly insect-hunters. Their tongues are very muscular and can shoot out in a split second. The sticky tip at the end grabs, holds on to, and then pulls in the prey.

Some of the larger chameleons also feed on small birds and mammals.

Crunch time

Once it has caught hold of an insect, the eyed lizard stuns the creature by shaking it violently from side to side. It then passes the insect to the back of its mouth, snaps its jaws together, and crushes the prey to bits.

Ah, meat!

The tegu lizard is a real meat-lover. Its diet includes young birds, mammals, and even fellow reptiles. Here, this tegu is tucking into an unfortunate rattlesnake. Mmm.

Enter the dragons

In the world of reptiles, dragons really do exist. These types of lizard often have incredible features that make them just as strange as the creatures found in fairy stories.

"Hey, watch the beard..."

This bearded dragon has a set of spiky scales around its throat, just like a man's beard. The "beard" expands so that the lizard will look too big for predators to swallow.

On the run

Most lizards get around on four legs, but – like people – the crested water dragon often uses just its two back (hind) legs when making a quick escape.

All talk, no action

If in danger, the frilled lizard opens its gaping mouth and spreads out an umbrella-like frill around its neck. This is to scare away any approaching predators.

Reptile file

● The eastern water dragon of Australia escapes from its enemies by diving underwater, where it can stay for up to 30 minutes.

● The frilled lizard's bright cape is a large flap of loose skin. When opened out, it can be more than four times the width of the lizard's body.

THE MANY-HEADED HYDRA

In Greek mythology, there was a terrible, dragon-like monster that haunted the marshes of Lerna, near Argos. This creature, known as the "Hydra", had nine heads and poisonous blood. Each time one of its heads was cut off in battle, a new one would grow in its place. The Hydra was eventually defeated by the warrior Hercules.

Komodo dragons can grow to nearly 3 m (10 ft) in length.

The lizard king

Komodo dragons are the largest of all living lizards. They can catch and kill goats and pigs, but often feed on the left-overs of dead animals.

17

Poisonous personalities

Some reptiles are "venomous". This means they are able to produce a poisonous fluid (venom) that can either be used for hunting or defence. A reptile's venom can paralyse its prey – or break down its blood and muscles, ready for eating.

Poisoning prey

Venomous snakes put poison into the body of their prey through hollow, stabbing teeth called fangs. The venom overpowers the victim and stops it from fighting back.

Nasty spit

All cobras have fixed fangs at the front of the mouth. Some use these for spitting venom into the face of their enemies – a defence strategy that can cause lots of pain, and even blindness.

Spitting black cobra

Spitting cobras can aim at enemy targets...

Fold-away fangs

Vipers have extra-long, hinged fangs that can be folded away when they are not needed. After stabbing their prey with the poisonous fangs, vipers "walk" their jaws from side to side – moving them further and further over the victim.

Vipers can move their folding fangs one at a time, like human fingers.

up to 2 m (6.5 ft) away.

THE MONSTER MUNCH

The Gila monster has venom glands in its lower jaw. It fools its prey by moving quite slowly until it is ready to strike. When it attacks, it turns very quickly and bites down violently. As it chews, the venom flows down grooves in its teeth and helps to kill the attacked animal.

Drooling dragons

The Komodo dragon is not venomous, but its spit contains many different types of bacteria. Even if a bitten animal manages to get away, it could still die of a nasty infection.

Venomous lizards

There are only two species of venomous lizard – the beaded lizard and the Gila ("heela") monster, below. Large rodents are their biggest prey.

Gila monster

19

Some like it hot

These reptiles are very skilled when it comes to handling the heat of the desert. They use the morning sunlight to warm up their bodies after a chilly night, and then hide away in bushes and burrows to escape the midday Sun.

Saving some for later

Desert lizards are good at coping with high temperatures. The spiny-tailed lizard (above) needs very little water, and stores extra food energy – in the form of fat – inside its chubby tail.

Smile and run

The collared lizard defends itself by trying to look as fierce as possible. It can give its enemies a nasty bite, if attacked, but prefers to scamper away to safety among the desert rocks.

A great sense of smell helps this lizard to find its food.

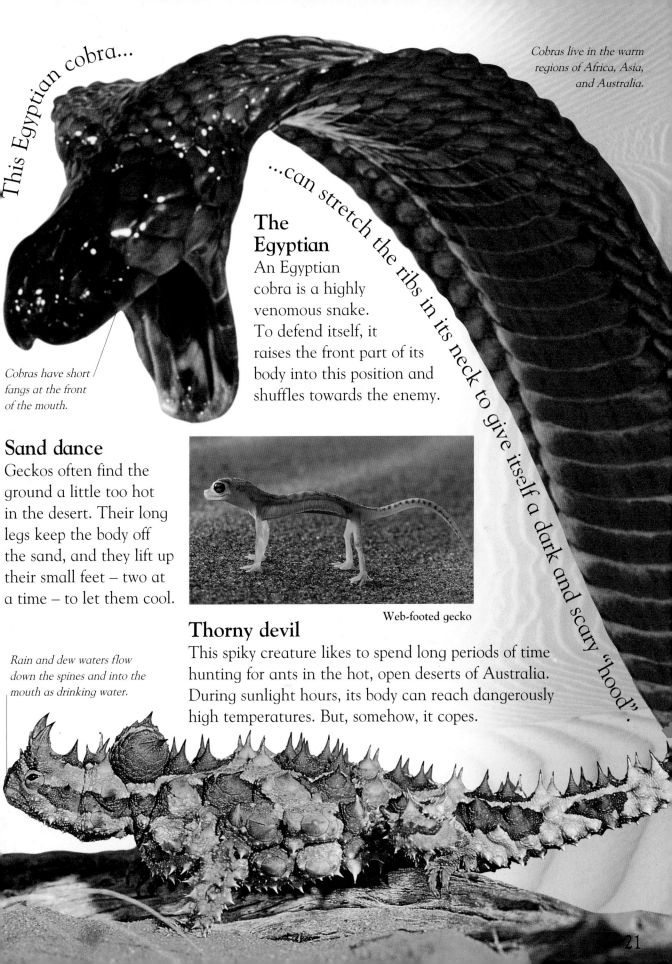

This Egyptian cobra...

Cobras live in the warm regions of Africa, Asia, and Australia.

...can stretch the ribs in its neck to give itself a dark and scary "hood".

Cobras have short fangs at the front of the mouth.

The Egyptian

An Egyptian cobra is a highly venomous snake. To defend itself, it raises the front part of its body into this position and shuffles towards the enemy.

Sand dance

Geckos often find the ground a little too hot in the desert. Their long legs keep the body off the sand, and they lift up their small feet – two at a time – to let them cool.

Web-footed gecko

Thorny devil

This spiky creature likes to spend long periods of time hunting for ants in the hot, open deserts of Australia. During sunlight hours, its body can reach dangerously high temperatures. But, somehow, it copes.

Rain and dew waters flow down the spines and into the mouth as drinking water.

Undercover

A lot of reptiles are very good at "camouflage" – the skill of blending into their natural surroundings. Camouflage is useful for avoiding enemies, as well as for sneaking up on prey without being seen.

Living logs

The swamps of Louisiana, USA, are full of alligators in disguise. Tiny algae (water plants) on the surface help to cover the gators so that they look like floating logs. They are actually hunting out their prey.

American alligators sometimes feed on prey as large as deer and cattle.

Colouring in

Cells in a chameleon's skin contain tiny grains of coloured "pigments". Sometimes, the pigments move around inside the cells, or areas of pigment get bigger and smaller. This causes the skin to change in colour.

A chameleon's skin colour usually keeps it hidden against the natural background.

Snake in the grass

The patterns on a gaboon viper's skin help to disguise the outline of its body. This makes it difficult to spot when it is hiding amongst leaf litter in the forests of tropical Africa.

BLACK AND BLUE MOODS

If a chameleon heats up, or moves into brighter sunlight, it may change colour. Changes in mood can also have an effect on its colour, such as if it is suddenly frightened. An angry chameleon may even turn black. These colour changes often make the chameleon very difficult to see.

Reptile "hide and seek" can be a matter of life and death.

Leaf-like lizard
Not all reptiles use just their colour or markings to blend in. Some, like this leaf-tailed gecko, also have body parts that are shaped like objects in their natural home.

Sssuch a good actor
Most predators prefer to eat living prey. So, if in danger, grass snakes often wriggle around as if they are dying. To finish, they turn over, curl up, lie still, and play dead.

I will survive

Running, hiding, and burrowing are good ways to avoid enemies. Over lots and lots of years, reptiles have developed many other fascinating methods of escape and self-defence.

A tail of escape

If caught by the tail, many lizards can get away by letting it break off. The bones in the tail have special cracks in them to allow this to happen. The tail will grow back during the next eight months.

Emerald tree skink

Lizards can use this tail trick more than once.

A sharper flavour

The armadillo lizard has a way of making its sharp, spiny body very difficult to attack and eat. Holding its tail in its mouth, it can curl its body into a prickly ball.

Horror show

Desert horned lizards use a strategy of surprise to defend themselves. They swell up in size and sometimes squirt blood from their eyes. Most attackers are so shocked they simply give up.

Kicking up a stink

To make up for its lack of size, the stinkpot turtle has to act quite aggressively when caught. It also defends itself by squirting out a really smelly scent (musk) from "stink glands" in the skin of its legs.

Leaps and bounds

Today, flying reptiles no longer exist – but a few remarkable reptiles have developed the ability to glide long distances through the air. Many reptiles can swim, but there is one that can walk on water!

These flaps of skin can be folded away when they are not needed.

Special features

Flying geckos have extra flaps of skin along the head, arms, legs, sides, and tail. As they jump from trees, the flaps spread out like parachutes. This slows the gecko into a graceful glide.

The gecko spreads its webbed toes as wide as possible for gliding.

The magician

The basilisk has a magical way of escaping danger. It can run across water. Its wide feet and broad, scaly toes help to keep it from sinking – but the real secret behind this trick is speed.

Free-falling

A flying snake cannot actually fly, but it can glide long distances from tree to tree. It usually takes off from a higher branch, and steers by twisting its body and using its tail as a rudder.

Flying snakes can drop right out of the danger zone.

The snake pulls in its belly to trap a layer of air, which cushions its fall.

Ready for take-off

This may sound like a fairy story, but flying dragons leap from tree to tree in the rainforests of Southeast Asia. They have a fine pair of colourful "wings", which they lift up when ready to glide.

Branch brigade

If a reptile species is "arboreal", it means that it spends most of its life in trees. Many arboreal reptiles have specially developed features for getting around their chosen habitat.

Superglue geckos

Geckos, like this tokay, are superb climbers. They have small, light bodies and grippy pads on their feet. The pads are covered in tiny, hair-like hooks that allow them to cling to all sorts of surfaces.

Anchor-tails

Tree snakes have extra-long tails for climbing. The tail coils around a branch and acts as an "anchor" while the snake hauls the rest of its body towards a higher level.

Geckos have five toes, which spread out to provide lots of grip for climbing.

Reptile file

● Arboreal lizards often have sharp claws for climbing tree trunks, as well as special pads for gripping on to silky leaves.

● The giant, or monkey-tailed, skink is the largest of the skink family. It can grow to 66 cm (26 in) in length.

Tree-dwelling
snakes use
the branches
and vines
as a leafy
disguise...

Shapes in the shadows

Skinks are known for their tube-shaped bodies
and cone-shaped heads. The giant skinks of
the Solomon Islands spend most of their time
in the trees, feeding on fruit and leaves by night.
In some parts of this region, humans eat them.

Fresh food

Some tree-dwelling
snakes lie in wait for
their meals, while
others are active
hunters. Cat-eyed
snakes are even quite
fond of swallowing
the eggs laid on
leaves by tree frogs.

Reptile realms

Reptiles are all over the place. They are found in almost every part of the world – except for the Arctic and Antarctic regions – but are more common in hot, lowland areas than in cooler, highland regions.

Pretty dangerous

Venomous eyelash pit vipers live in the rainforests of Central and South America. The raised scales around their big, bulging eyes make them look like they have long, pretty eyelashes.

Reptile file

● Over time, many reptiles have adapted to life in villages, towns, and cities.

● Moving around in hot, dry areas uses up a lot of water and energy – so desert reptiles are mainly active at night.

● Mountain peaks and polar regions are the only places without reptiles.

Sun worshippers

Most lizards are well-adapted to hot, dry conditions. Agama lizards make their homes in the grasslands or scrublands of Africa, where they can sun themselves to heat their bodies.

Grasping, prehensile tail.

Tree boas hang down head-first

Coiled climber

Tree boas are good climbers, with a "prehensile" tail that grips and holds branches tightly. Longer and slimmer than ground boas, they can slide easily through the branches.

...and use sharp teeth to seize a good meal.

Holiday homes

Land iguanas are often found in tropical settings, where they can bask on rocks near the coast. This rock iguana (left) is taking it easy in the Bahamas.

Housemates

Lots of reptiles use underground burrows – but often for different reasons. Tortoises use them to escape hot, dry weather, skinks to run away from predators, and snakes to hunt burrowing mammals.

The hardbacks

Chelonians all have one thing in common – the hard-shell home they carry around. Every reptile in this group has a set of hardy features that help it to cope with its natural environment.

Giant tortoises have shells up to 1.3 m (4 ft) long.

Island wonder

The giant tortoises of the Galápagos Islands are not bothered by the hot, dry conditions there. They live on bare, rocky ground and can go without food and water for long periods of time.

Reptile file

• Tortoises and turtles can live for more than 100 years.

• The "growth rings" on a *Chelonian*'s bony plates help to show how old it is.

• Some turtles can survive for weeks underwater without having to come up for air.

Hard house

Chelonian shells are made of a dome-shaped top and a flatter shield under the belly. Both parts are made up of bony plates. The surface of the shell is covered in large scales called scutes.

Domed top (carapace).

Shielded belly (plastron).

Bottoms up!

Turtles push their head above water to take in air, but can also breathe underwater. They do this by taking air in through their skin, the lining of their throat, and also through a small hole near their bottom!

European pond turtle

The giant tortoise's long neck helps it to reach up to high-growing plants.

Heads up!

Most *Chelonians* are able to pull their heads back into their shells for protection. If involved in a squabble, they bring their heads right out to show their anger.

These two giant tortoises are having a bit of an argument.

Shell suits

The shells are needed for self-defence. High-arched and knobbly shells give protection from bad weather and predators. Shells that blend into the natural surroundings can also help to disguise tortoises and turtles.

Snake-neck turtle

Starred tortoise

Alligator snapping turtle

Pond turtle (terrapin)

Sea monsters

Many reptiles are suited to ocean life. Some have a powerful heart that keeps the blood pumping during deep dives in cold water, and glands to remove sea salt from their bodies.

The wetter the better

Sea snakes have a flattened tail, which they use as a paddle for moving in water – a bit like a boat's oar. They are superb swimmers, but find it extremely difficult to get around on land.

The back feet are used for steering – like the rudder on a boat.

Slick and quick

These sea turtles have large front flippers and light, flat, smoothly-shaped shells. Such features help them to move quickly through water. Some can reach speeds of up to 29 kmh (18 mph).

Green sea turtles

The flipper-shaped front legs help the turtle to glide through water.

Tough at the top

Most turtles have hard, plated shells on their backs, but – as its name suggests – the giant leatherback turtle is different. It has a tough-looking shell made of thick, leathery skin.

Reptile file

● Sea snakes are the most poisonous snakes in the world.

● Sea turtles cry salty tears. This is to get rid of the extra, unwanted salt they swallow as they swim and feed.

● The leatherback turtle can grow to 1.8 m (6 ft) in length.

Seaweed feeding
The marine iguana of the Galápagos Islands is the only lizard in the world that swims and feeds in the sea. Other sea creatures need not be afraid, though, as this monster of the deep is definitely a vegetarian. It only eats seaweed.

The marine iguana likes to sunbathe on rocks between visits to the sea.

Snap

These snappy-looking creatures are large, intelligent reptiles that are well-adapted to life in the water. *Crocodilians* all have similar features, but there are some interesting differences, too.

The strange bump on a male's snout is called a ghara.

A gharial's teeth are all the same size and shape.

Air conditioning

A crocodile uses various tricks to control its body temperature. On a hot day, it can cool down by raising its head and opening its mouth – or by crawling away into the shade or into water.

Crocodiles are more closely related to birds than to other reptiles.

Nile crocodile

Snack attack

All *Crocodilian* reptiles are meat-eaters (carnivores). Even the larger crocs and gators are quick and strong enough to launch themselves out of the water – straight up into the air like a rocket – and snatch their prey.

Ganges
gharial

Scissor-face

It is easy to recognise a gharial by the shape of its head.
It has a long snout and scissor-like jaws that each contain
more than 50 teeth. This kind of head is excellent for fishing.

Gator or croc?

Alligators are not as
widespread as crocodiles.
They only live in south-
eastern USA and China.
Gators have a shorter body
and snout than crocs – but
they usually live longer.

American alligator

Alligator junior

This is a caiman – a type of alligator from Central
and South America. The caiman is smaller than other
Crocodilians and can move much
more quickly on land. Its body
is protected by strong,
bony plates.

*A crocodile's fourth
tooth sticks out when
its mouth is closed.*

*Caiman teeth are sharper and
longer than alligator teeth.*

37

Croc characters

The creatures of the *Crocodilia* group are related to reptiles that lived more than 200 million years ago. These dinosaur relatives are fierce, dangerous predators – but they also have a good social life and make surprisingly caring parents.

Ready salted

The saltwater crocodile, or "saltie", is one of the few crocs to inhabit saltwater, although it also lives in freshwater rivers and lakes. Salties have large salt glands on the back of their tongue to get rid of the extra, unwanted salt.

MONSTER OF THE DEEP

Saltwater crocodiles can stay underwater for more than an hour. This kind of croc is the largest reptile alive today, and one of the world's most powerful animals. It is strong enough to kill and eat a human. The "saltie" lives over a wide area, from southern India to Fiji in the Pacific Ocean, and has been seen hundreds of kilometres from the nearest land.

Ancient reptiles

The dinosaurs belonged to a group of creatures called the *Archosaurs*, or "ruling reptiles". *Crocodilian* reptiles also belong to this family – in fact, they are the only *Archosaurs* still alive.

Crocodile skull from dinosaur period.

Skull and jaws of a modern crocodile.

Reptile file

● Croc mothers lay between 10 and 90 eggs at a time.

● The largest crocs can grow to more than 7 m (23 ft) long.

● Adult crocs swallow rocks to help them break up (digest) their food.

● Some crocodiles can live for up to 100 years.

Dwarf of the riverbank

Dwarf crocodiles are the smallest species of croc, and grow to just 2 m (6.5 ft) long. They are shy, secretive animals that hide away in riverbank holes when in danger.

Dwarf crocodile

Careful crocs

A female croc carries her newly-hatched young to the water inside her mouth. She can carry as many as 15 in one go. This is very important for the babies' survival.

Croc courtship

To attract a mate, male *Crocodilians* lift up their heads and bellow. The noise helps to warn off rival males. They also blow bubbles in the water to win the attention of females.

Nile crocodile

Little devils

Like most animals, male and female reptiles mate to produce offspring. Reptiles are usually born on land. Most hatch from waterproof eggs, while a few are born as live young.

Chips off the old block

Whether hatchlings or live young, reptile babies usually look like miniature versions of their parents. The baby leopard tortoise will develop its darker, adult markings as it grows up.

She's mine, she's mine!

As the mating season begins, male monitors often wrestle one another. The fight is just a "display" for attracting a female mate, and the weaker lizard usually gives up before either one gets hurt.

The not so great escape

Snakes lay eggs with soft, leathery shells. The hatchlings have a special "egg" tooth, which they use to tear a hole in the shell – but it can take up to two days for a baby snake to fully emerge.

Reptiles with fewer young make the more caring parents.

Reptile file

- Most reptiles leave their young to look after themselves.

- Lizards and snakes that hatch inside the body of the mother usually have a greater chance of survival.

- Marine turtles can lay as many as 200 eggs in one go.

Ready-made babes

Lots of snakes and lizards give birth to live young – just like human beings do – rather than laying eggs. They emerge in little membrane sacks, but escape from these very quickly.

Safety in the sea

Female turtles make nests in the sand – using their back flippers – where they will lay very large groups (clutches) of eggs. Once hatched, the young turtles make their way directly to the sea. Here, they will be less at risk from attack.

Eggs are laid on land so that the babies can get oxygen from the air.

41

Swamp things

Swamps are found in many different parts of the world. They are areas of boggy land covered in still or slow-moving water. Plants and trees grow in and around the swamps, making them an ideal kingdom for reptiles.

This bite has venom
Unlike most venomous snakes, the mangrove snake has fangs at the back of its mouth. This means that it chews and poisons its prey at the same time.

The big-headed mangrove snake has jaws that are wide enough...

...to swallow birds' eggs

...or even squirrels.

Swampland swimmers

The bendy body of a snake, such as this garter snake, helps to make it a good swimmer. It can glide through the water by moving its body from side to side in S-shaped curves.

Stretch and snap

A snapping turtle does not have to move fast to catch its food – its stretchy neck and violent bite will do all the work. This miniature monster will eat anything it can fit between its jaws!

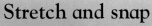

A safer place

Green iguanas find that the tree branches around mangrove swamps are great places for sunbathing. Their leafy-green colouring hides them from predators – so they can relax.

Green iguanas use their tail for swimming, and as a defensive whip.

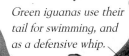

A FISHING LESSON

The largest freshwater turtle in the Americas is the alligator snapping turtle (see page 33), which "fishes" for its food. It lies in wait with its sharp, beak-like jaws wide open. There is a pink bulge on its tongue that looks like a fisherman's worm – this is the bait that attracts fish, which then have no escape as the jaws quickly snap shut.

Reptiles have a long history – their relatives date back to the days of the dinosaurs. Crocodiles are the closest-living relatives of the dinosaurs, but they were not the first reptiles to inhabit our world.

The fossilized remains of a prehistoric turtle.

Turtle power

Turtles have lived on Earth longer than any other group of reptiles. Their distant relatives may have been around at the same time as the very first dinosaurs.

Tuatara time

Although there are not many of them about today, tuataras certainly stick around for a long time. They reach adulthood at the age of 20, but are still growing at 60, and can live to be 120 years old.

LAST OF THE BEAK-HEADS

The reptiles of the *Rhynchocephalia* group, or "Beak-head" reptiles, were plentiful during the age of the dinosaurs – but today, the tuatara is the only species left in the group. Tuataras are relatives of the *Homeosaurus* – a similar-looking creature from the same group – that lived about 140 million years ago.

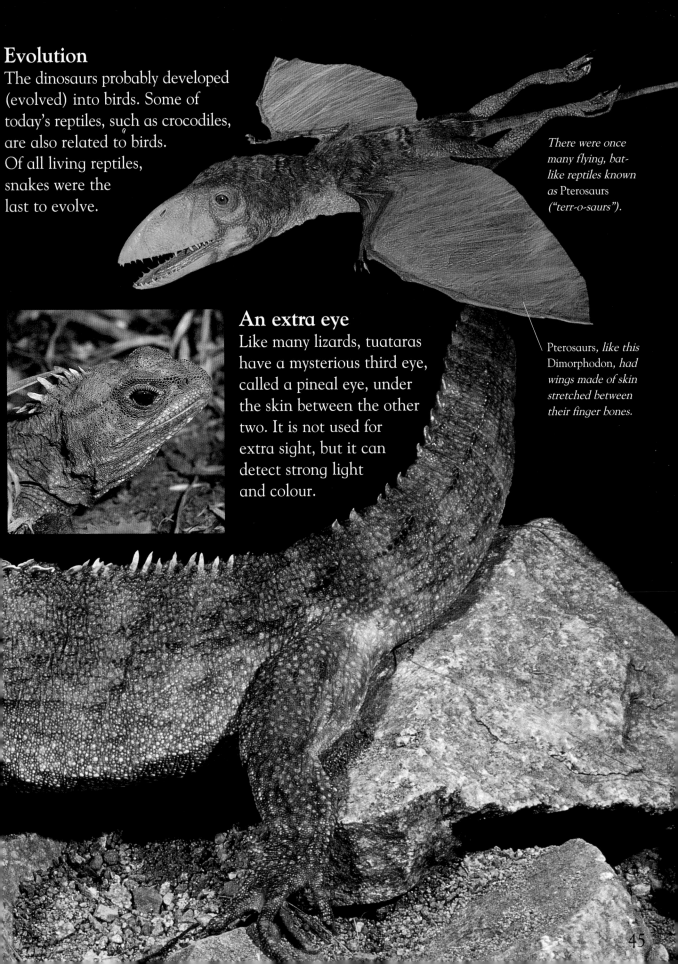

Evolution

The dinosaurs probably developed (evolved) into birds. Some of today's reptiles, such as crocodiles, are also related to birds. Of all living reptiles, snakes were the last to evolve.

There were once many flying, bat-like reptiles known as Pterosaurs ("terr-o-saurs").

An extra eye

Like many lizards, tuataras have a mysterious third eye, called a pineal eye, under the skin between the other two. It is not used for extra sight, but it can detect strong light and colour.

Pterosaurs, *like this* Dimorphodon, *had wings made of skin stretched between their finger bones.*

Reptile glossary

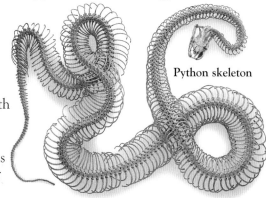

Python skeleton

Arboreal creatures that live in trees or spend a lot of time there.

Backbone (spine) a flexible chain of bones running down an animal's back. Animals with a backbone, such as reptiles, are called vertebrates.

Camouflage the way animals hide by blending in with their natural surroundings.

Clutch a number of eggs all laid at the same time.

Cold-blooded an animal that uses its natural surroundings to warm up or cool down.

Dinosaurs prehistoric reptiles that once ruled the world, but died out 65 million years ago.

Display showing off parts of the body to attract a mate or defend a territory.

Evolution over very long periods of time, all creatures develop (evolve) different skills and features that help them to cope with, or adapt to, their habitat. This is known as evolution.

Freshwater freshwater habitats are watery homes that are not salty, such as ponds and rivers.

Glands parts of an animal's body that can squeeze out substances such as venom, sweat, stinky musk, and salt.

Habitat the natural home and surroundings of a living creature.

Hatchlings the name for baby animals that emerge from eggs.

Jacobson's organ a sense organ in the mouth of snakes and lizards, which allows them to "smell" and "taste" their surroundings using their tongues.

Keratin a horny substance that forms strong, flexible fibres and makes up part of a reptile's scales.

Mating season a period when male and female animals mate to produce new offspring (young).

Moulting or sloughing getting rid of (shedding) old skin and scales.

Order a grouping of related animal types (species).

Pigment a substance inside body cells, such as skin cells, that produces colour.

Pineal eye the name for the small, "third eye" that many lizards have.

Predator an animal that hunts and eats other animals.

Prehensile body parts, such as a coiled tail, that are good at gripping on to things.

Prey an animal that is hunted and eaten by other animals (predators).

Saltwater saltwater habitats are places such as seas, oceans, and river estuaries.

Scales the thin, overlapping, waterproof plates that cover a reptile's skin.

Scutes the large, tough, horny scales – such as those on tortoise and turtle shells, snakes' bellies, and the armoured skin of *Crocodilians*.

Senses the five main senses are eyesight, hearing, smell, touch, and taste – but some snakes can also sense heat.

Skeleton the bony framework that supports and protects an animal's body.

Species a group of animals that share similar characteristics (features) and breed together to produce fertile young.

Venom a poisonous liquid that some reptiles (mainly snakes) use for hunting or self-defence.

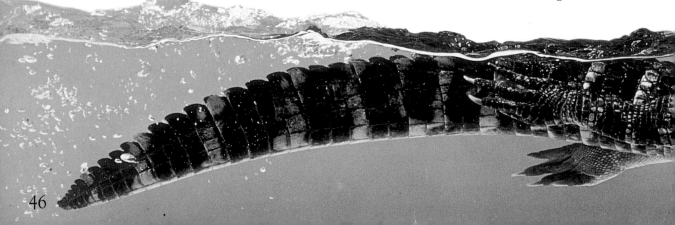

Reptile habitats

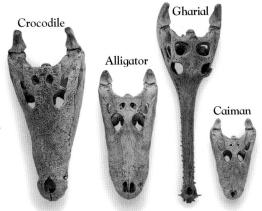

Crocodile

Alligator

Gharial

Caiman

African egg-eating snake pg. 11
Most habitats in central and southern Africa, south of the Sahara Desert.

American alligator pgs. 22, 37, 47
Freshwater swamps, lakes, and rivers in south-eastern North America.

Armadillo girdled lizard pg. 25
Rocky outcrops and scrublands (areas of dry land) in South Africa and Namibia.

Basilisk lizard pg. 26
By rivers in the tropical rainforests of Central America.

Bearded dragon pg. 16
Dry forests and deserts in eastern central Australia.

Boa constrictor pg. 13
Rainforests, dry woodlands, and places near to human homes in Central and South America.

Cat-eyed snake pgs. 28, 29
Semi-dry scrublands in Central and South America.

Collared lizard pg. 20
Semi-dry places in the west of North America.

Crested water dragon pg. 16
River-filled forests in Southeast Asia.

Desert horned lizard pg. 25
Hot, sandy deserts in North America.

Desert tortoise pg. 4
Dry scrublands, meadows, and sand dunes in southern Europe, northern Africa, and western Asia.

Dwarf crocodile pg. 39
Rainforest swamps, ponds, and slow-moving rivers in Africa.

Egyptian cobra pg. 21
Grasslands (open, grassy plains), dry woodlands, and areas around the edge of the Sahara Desert in North Africa, plus the Middle East, and Arabia.

European eyed lizard pg. 15
Open woodlands, vineyards, and olive groves in France, Italy, Spain, and Portugal.

Flying dragon pg. 27
The rainforests of Southeast Asia.

Frilled (neck) lizard pg. 16
Savanna woodlands in northern Australia and southern New Guinea.

Galápagos giant tortoise pgs. 32, 33
Rocky, volcanic areas of the Galápagos Islands in the Pacific Ocean.

Galápagos marine iguana pg. 35
Rocky shorelines of the Galápagos Islands. Feeds in the sea.

Gila monster pg. 19
Deserts and dry grasslands in south-western USA (North America).

Green anaconda pg. 13
Rainforest rivers, lagoons, and flooded grasslands in South America.

Green iguana pg. 43
River-filled forests in Mexico and South America.

Jackson's three-horned chameleon pg. 15
High, mountainous forests in Kenya and Tanzania.

Komodo dragon pgs. 17, 19
The grasslands and woodlands of only a few islands in Indonesia.

Leaf-tailed gecko pg. 23
Rainforests in eastern Madagascar.

Leatherback turtle pgs. 34, 41
Temperate and tropical oceans throughout the world.

Mitre sandfish (skink) pgs. 6, 31
The deserts and grassy plains (or "steppes") of western Arabia.

Namib web-footed gecko pg. 21
Sandy areas in south-western Africa.

Nile crocodile pgs. 4, 36, 39
Rivers and lakes in Africa and Madagascar.

Pond turtle (terrapin) pg. 33
Still or slow-moving freshwater habitats in Europe, Africa, and Asia.

Red-foot tortoise pg. 6
Grasslands and savanna woodlands in northern South America.

Rock iguana pg. 31
Dry, rocky habitats on tropical islands near to the Americas.

Snake-neck turtle pg. 33
Slow-moving rivers, streams, swamps, and lagoons in eastern Australia.

Spectacled caiman pgs. 6, 37
Lakes, rivers, and swamps in Central and South America.

Starred tortoise pg. 33
Deserts and dry habitats in southern Asia.

Stinkpot turtle (or musk turtle) pg. 25
Lakes, ponds, and rivers in North America.

Tegu lizard pg. 15
Forests and grasslands near to the Amazon and Orinoco rivers in South America.

Thorny devil (or moloch) pg. 21
Deserts in western and central Australia.

Tokay gecko pg. 28
Forests and human habitats in Southeast Asia.

Tuatara pgs. 5, 44, 45
The rocky areas of islands near to New Zealand in the Pacific Ocean.

Western diamondback rattlesnake pg. 10
Deserts, scrublands, and dry woodlands in southern USA and northern Mexico.

American alligator

Index

Red-tailed racer

Acknowledgements

Dorling Kindersley would like to thank:
Dorian Spencer Davies for original artwork illustrations, and Rachel Hilford, Sally Hamilton, and Sarah Mills for DK Picture Library research.

Picture Credits

(Key: a = above; c = centre; b = below; l = left; r = right; t = top)
The publisher would like to thank the following for their kind permission to reproduce their photographs:

BBC Natural History Unit: Pete Oxford 31cra; Tony Phelps 25; Michael Pitts 19cr; David Welling 18bl. **Bruce Coleman Ltd:** Andres Blomqvist 8-9; Gerald S Cubitt 45cla. **Corbis:** 318; Jonathan Blair 36bl; Stephen Fink 37cra; Patricia Fogden 29bc; Gallo Images 39bc; Joe McDonald 8tl, 39cr. **FLPA – Images of nature:** Robin Chittenden 13bc; Michael Gore 31clb; David Hosking 14; Chris Mattison 11ca; Minden Pictures 32-33. **Chris Mattison Nature Photographics:** Chris Mattison 6-7. **N.H.P.A.:** ANT 38, 40cla; Anthony Bannister 18bc, 26bl; G I Bernard 4-5; Laurie Campbell 40bc; Martin Harvey 8cl, 39cla; Daniel Heuclin 15bc, 19cla, 29ca; Hellion & Van Ingen 33cra. **Oxford Scientific Films:** Daniel J Cox 3; David B Fleetham 41; Michael Fogden 23tr, 30; Jim Frazier / Mantis Wildlife Films 21bc; Olivier Grunewald 41bc; Howard Hall 34cla, 35; Mike Hill 20tr; John Mitchel 36cla; Raymond A Mendez / Animals Animals 25tr; Zig Leszcynski 44-45, 11tl, 25crb; Srtan Osolinski 31tl; Tui de Roy 33c; Tom Ulrich 5ca. **Premaphotos Wildlife:** Ken Preston-Mafham 27crb. **Science Photo Library:** Gregory Dimijian 1; Tom McHugh 18ca; John Mitchell 12tc; Jany Sauvanet 34clb. **Woodfall Wild Images:** Bob Gibbons 37tr; Heinrich van den Berg 21c; David Woodfall 22ca.

Jacket images – back cover:
Corbis: Stephen Frink.

All other images: © Dorling Kindersley. For further information, see www.dkimages.com